What People are S

MW00683169

Willis speaks frankly about his own search for God and how all the "right" things—including seminary—left him feeling empty. With compassion and humility, he shares the practical ideas and helpful illustrations that God used to draw him into a life-giving relationship. If you're disillusioned with doctrine and want to connect with the Living God, this book is a great starting place.
--**JM**, Massachusetts

Dad always said, "a good teacher is one who can take apparently complex issues and explain them to a six year old, without loss of content." Willis is such a teacher. He cuts through silly religious language, "we understand what we are talking about; don't we?" He exposes obscure and incorrect church doctrine and obtuse alleged principles which are either misunderstood or do not actually exist at all. Thank You Brother.
--**FO**, South Carolina

Wonderful! Seems one never tires of reading truth as it is presented. It is a moment of reality in this otherwise muddy world of religion and theology.
--**PM,** Wisconsin

Thank you so much for your manuscript!! We printed it out at church and I am currently reading it. How wonderful that you've taken the time to write all your thoughts into a book. I am greatly enjoying reading it and meditating on your words, and just wanted you to know we have indeed received your labor of love and are being blessed through it.
--**DB & MB,** Nebraska

I just got it! It came in the mail this morning. You really nailed it; I love everything about this book; I can't put it down. Could you send me two more copies? I don't want to let mine go anywhere. What a blessing and a joy to revisit our past walk together written in a book I can hold in my hands. Thank you from the bottom of my nephish and chaiim. (Editorial comment: This refers to two Hebrew words for "life" used in the book).
--**ES**, New Mexico

I just finished the book last evening, it is a wonderful work that will give many new life. Your book captures the essence of the Christian walk and it will change many lives. I am so excited about this book and so glad you finally did it; your ministry will live on long after you have gone home.
--**PR**, Montana

3D Christianity
and the Nesses

Exploring the missing dimension of
the Christian walk and providing
eight spiritual practices for Christian
transformation

Willis Larson

3D Christianity and the Nesses

Willis A. Larson
1213 Salem Street
North Andover, MA 01845

All Scripture, unless otherwise noted, is taken from the New American Standard Bible, Copyright 1960, 1962,1963,1968,1971,1972,1973,1975, 1977,1995 by The Lockman Foundation. Used by permission.

ISBN: 978-0-9846650-1-3
    1.   Spiritual life – Christianity. 2.Spiritual exercises. 3. Spiritual
        transformation.
Library of Congress Card Number:
Printed in the United States of America

07 08 09 10 11 12⁵ 12 11 10 9 8 7 6 5 4

Acknowledgements

First of all, I want to thank the many saints who have walked with us over the years while the Holy Spirit was writing this book into our lives. In various places and times they have been the Church, loving us, supporting us and encouraging us in our walk. In that sense, this is "our" book.

I want to thank Trudy, my loving wife for all her encouragement to create this book and for all her support and patience over the summer while I was in the writing mode.

Also, I want to thank Julia Maranan for her careful and thoughtful comments and editing on her three passes through the manuscript. And many thanks to Steve and Jan Koenig for their helpful and extensive feedback and for Jan's excellent editing on the first comprehensive edit.

I am truly grateful to the several others who have taken time from their busy schedules to read and comment on the manuscript while it was in preparation. My thanks to Andrea Lerman, who prayerfully read and meditated on the work and who made the trip to our home to spend considerable time sharing from her perspective as a spiritual director. My thanks to Paul Harmon who also came to our home with insightful questions and comments as a keen observer of culture and a fellow engineering-type. Thanks also to Paul and Pauline Marker for their helpful input. My thanks to Benny Parish for his faithful friendship and for his great overall input- especially his comments on the Forgiveness chapter.

And last, but certainly not least, to Elizabeth, my daughter and princess, in spite of her very busy schedule, for all her loving labor, patient support, and incredible insight on the final editing passes through the manuscript.

They have truly added to the tone and tenor of this book.

To Trudy
My Loving and Faithful Companion
in the Walk of Life

CONTENTS

A Short Note to My Readers

 This book consists of two sections: "3D Christianity" followed by "The Nesses."

May I suggest you read the whole book first to get a feeling for its contents. Then, I would suggest that you find a quiet space and a nice cup of tea to begin an extended second reading. The message here is quite dense and requires some time and prayer to process properly. It is written to be read and used in small bites, alternating between reading a little from the 3D Christianity section and then a little from the Nesses section.

Read it prayerfully, so that its contents are not acquired just as head knowledge. It is not my intention to teach the principles and truths of Jesus Christ; rather I pray that as you read it you will meet the One Who Is the Truth in a life-changing way and that He would bring His peace and His joy to you in reading.

I would encourage you to hold what you read before the Lord and pray, " Lord, if I don't need this part, let it fall to the ground. If I don't need this part *for now*, put it on the shelf until You are ready to place it into my life. Or if it *is* for me right now, put it into my heart and allow me to experience You in it." I pray that you might be given His eyes to see and His ears to hear and His heart to understand, that you might touch the Living God.

Introduction

The Christian Community

A growing number of evangelical Christians know that there is something wrong in the organized church and in the Christian community at large. We feel unease in our souls and see a huge gap when comparing the Church in the Bible with what we see in the contemporary Christian community.

It saddens me when I observe that the evangelical Christian community is seriously fractured and is virtually indistinguishable from the secular culture.

Several years ago I was doing a conference in the Midwest for a group of Christians I had known for many years. During the conference I brought up the sad state of contemporary Christianity at large here in North America.

I shared with them that for more than 40 years, as I studied the evangelical Christian community, I was continually struck with how powerless and fractured it was. In the early 1960s, while I was in seminary, I studied the 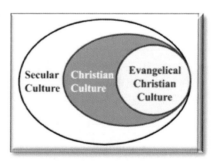 history of one Pentecostal denomination that was born out of a sovereign work of God in 1904 called the Welsh revival, and the subsequent Azusa Street Revival in Los Angeles (1906 to 1915). This denomination was formally organized by 1914, and in the following 50 years, it fragmented into more than 150 other separate denominations, all over differences of theology and doctrine.

I showed them an article[1] by the consulting group ReligiousTolerance.org reporting that as of 2006 it counted more than 1,500 (yes, 1,500; it is not a typo) separate denominations in North America.

Then, I shared that the incidence of pornography was about the same for the evangelical Christian culture as for the secular culture. For example, in 2003, Focus on the Family did a poll showing that:

- 47% of respondents said pornography is a problem in their home,
- 50% of men viewed pornography within one week of attending a Promise Keepers stadium event, and
- 54% of pastors said they had viewed pornography within the past year.

And, I shared with them that the incidence of divorce within the church is grater that that in the secular society.

In turn, many in the group shared their sadness over the abuse they had observed and experienced within the church organization , sighting rampant bickering, backbiting, power politics, bitterness and unforgiveness, just to name a few items.

---

[1] Article available at http://www.religioustolerance.org/chr_deno.htm.

During my observations over those 40 years, I concluded that much of the evangelical Christian community is indiscernible from the secular culture; it has just as much sickness and disease, anger, bitterness, backbiting, accusation, envy, jealousy, fear, stress, anxiety, depression, dissension, strife, abuse, divorce, abortion, and pornography as is found in secular culture.

One of the attendees said to me, "Will, you are being way too hard on the Church." My response was, "Brother, what part of what I have said is not true? We need to be concerned about the sad state of Christianity today. The Christian culture is a reflection of the lives of the individual Christians that make up the culture." It is clear that the Christian community is in trouble. We, as members of the Christian community, need radical change. We need transformation.

Chapter Nine Problem

Many books we read today have what I call the "chapter nine problem." The first six to eight chapters are a really helpful hard-hitting analysis, spelling out the problem. We agree with the analysis and now we're fired up and ready to move into the chapters that share the solution and help us get involved. But alas…that chapter or those chapters are lacking or missing altogether. I call this the "chapter nine problem." It is not my intent to expound further in this book on the problems within the Christian community. In this book I want to go immediately to chapter nine and explore how an ordinary Christian can participate in the Christian life as God intended from the beginning. The solution to the problem is not organizational—it is an individual heart solution. I believe the solution lies in our learning to live in the third dimension of Christianity and practicing the "Nesses" – giving God permission to do His work in us, changing us into the likeness of His Son, Jesus and allowing Him to manifest His life in our walk.

> **Learn to live in the third dimension of Christianity, practicing the "Nesses." Give God permission to do His work, changing us into the likeness of His Son, Jesus and allow Him to manifest His life in our walk.**

God in This Book

When I use the word "God" or the words "Father God" or "heavenly Father" in this book, I am referring to the triune Father, Son, and the Holy Spirit; the God of Abraham, Isaac, and Jacob. While it is true that Father God is in heaven with Jesus His Son sitting (or standing) at his right hand, it is also true that the Father is in the Son and the Son is in the Spirit (John 15) and the Spirit comes to dwell in the spirit of all those who have invited Him into their lives. God in heaven can seem like a very-long-distance call; God indwelling in our spirit is immediately available. Touch Him in your spirit as you read. Allow Him to show you Himself.

The Heart in This Book

When I refer to the *heart* in this book, I am speaking of your spiritual heart. In the Scriptures, the heart can refer to the physical blood pump made of flesh, it can refer to the soul, or it can mean the innermost core of a person, which is the soul plus the spirit—that is,  everything of you that is not your physical being. In this book I call this innermost core of a person the "spiritual heart."

Later in this book I will explain in more detail that the soul of man is the mind, the will, and the emotions. The spirit is not the same as the soul. For a Christian (one who has invited God to come into his or her life), the spirit is the dwelling place of God.

When I suggest that you engage your heart, I am not suggesting that you "think about it," or "emote about it," or just "will it to happen." I am suggesting that you center yourself (your mind, will, and emotions) in the place where God dwells, in your inner core; center yourself in His presence in your spirit and allow Him to have control. **[Puppyness]**[2] Give God permission to give you His eyes to see, His ears to hear, and His Heart to understand and experience what is happening. The matter of the heart will become clearer as you read further in this book.

---

[2] A word in square brackets refers to one of the Nesses in the second section

Scope of This Book

As Christians, we are called to the dual tasks of *restoration* and *transformation*

1) *Restoration:* To be restored to humanity's initial state in the Garden of Eden by removing the enemy's kingdom from our lives.
2) *Transformation:* To be transformed by God's indwelling life and a walk of obedience, being changed into the likeness of Jesus Christ.

Restoration is God's plan to redeem the fall of man. The fall in the garden did not come as a surprise to God—He had foreseen it even before the foundations of the  Earth and had made provisions in Himself to make the way of recovery possible. Because of the finished work of Jesus Christ on the cross in complete obedience to His heavenly Father, we are able to remove the enemy and his kingdom from our lives and to deal with the consequences of sin.

But wait! Recovery is not enough; it just restores us to a place where we can now enter into God's initial and eternal purpose for his creation in the garden: that we would be *transformed* into His likeness, from shadow into reality. His purpose has not changed. We are called to a dependent, intimate walk of obedience, eating continually of the Tree of Life, which is the person of Jesus Christ. This includes being born again, to restore the life of God in us, and receiving the empowering of the Holy Spirit to enable us to walk the Christian Life in dependent obedience.

Restoration and transformation are absolutely foundational to our walk as Christians. It is important to understand that restoration is not transformation. Removing the enemy from our lives does not change us into the likeness of Jesus Christ; it just returns us to the state of Adam and Eve in the garden before the fall. We still must receive the Life of God (being born again) and the baptism of the Holy Spirit (empowerment) and live a life of obedience to the Person of God in order to be changed into His likeness. In the normal Christian life, we do not need to wait until we are restored to begin transformation; we can expect both restoration and transformation to be happening simultaneously.

This book focuses on the process of transformation. More information on restoration can be found on our website, www.beingchanged.com.

3D Christianity

Exploring the missing
dimension of the
Christian walk

2D Christianity

Books and Books

Several years ago, as I was surfing the Internet, I came across the website of a large local Christian bookseller. Its homepage indicated that it had more than 150,000 books in 30 different categories. If you visited its warehouse, there was shelving forty feet high as far as the eye could see in all directions. As engineers do, I did some math and calculated that this amounted to more than one million words written for each and every significant word in the Bible! I asked myself, "Why do we need so many Christian books?"

Christians Are Not Satisfied

Not long ago a young man said to me, "I come from a very conservative background. All my life I have studied the Bible and heard the sermons. My head is full of knowledge but my heart is still empty."

My observation is that most Christians are not satisfied in their walk, and because they are not satisfied, they search and search to satisfy their spiritual hunger. Many read book after book, attend conference after conference, watch and listen to hour after hour of TV and radio preachers and gospel music, hoping for something that will satisfy their souls.

And, as they expand that search, many go into new-age and occult practices and new religions for answers. This dissatisfaction and hunger usually comes from large gaping holes in their Christian foundation. They may know the Bible, theology, principles, and doctrine and they are often very busy doing good works for God, but still they are not satisfied; something is missing.

What is missing is a significant day-to-day relationship with God, a real relationship that provides the sense of His presence, His peace, His joy and a hope and purpose for life.

> **What is missing is a significant day-by-day relationship with God, a real relationship that provides the sense of His presence, His peace, His joy and a hope and purpose for life.**

The Two Lines

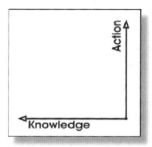

One day as I considered the sad state of the Christian community, the Lord showed me a picture, an illustration of two lines meeting in space. Think of it as a piece of paper with two lines drawn on it (see diagram at left). The two lines meet at the bottom right corner. The horizontal line represents "Knowledge" and the vertical line represents "Action." As you may recall from high school geometry, these two lines intersecting in space form a plane. Label this plane (the sheet of paper) "The Christian Culture."

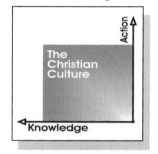

Knowledge Line: Many in the Christian community are very much into knowledge—they spend a great deal of time and energy pursuing theology, doctrines, principles, Bible study, charts and graphs, time lines, and maps, etc. There are hundreds of thousands of books and billions of words published, all about God. This is piling up knowledge upon knowledge.

Action Line: Others in the Christian community are very much into action, doing programs and projects without end, striving to bring about the Kingdom of God by all their activity and good works; they are very busy "doing good stuff for God."

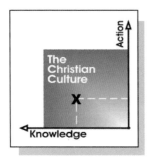

I discovered that one could define almost any Christian organization in terms of these two parameters, knowledge and action. Referring to the diagram on the left, this shows an example of an organization (the "X" shown) that is about half into knowledge and about one-third into action.

Now take the plane (piece of paper) and turn it so you are viewing it "on edge." Mathematically speaking, this plane in fact does not exist. The lines disappear, and, therefore, the plane disappears. The plane is only two-dimensional: it has no thickness, no depth, no substance.

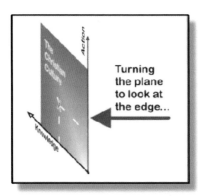

Turning the plane to look at the edge...

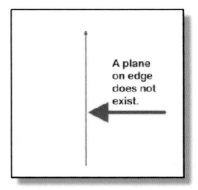

A plane on edge does not exist.

The two lines, Knowledge and Action, are just empty religion – the religion of knowing *about* God and doing good for God. Two dimensional religion does not change you into the image of Jesus Christ. Nothing of eternal significance happens in two dimensional Christianity. Why is the heart still empty? It is because the third dimension of the Christian walk is missing.

The Third Dimension

The Life Dimension
Suggested Reading: John 15, Romans 8:28f

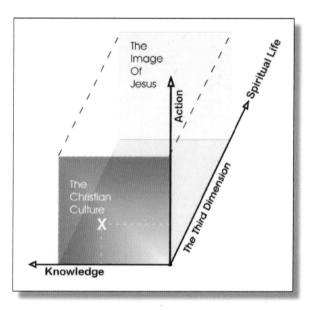

The missing third dimension is illustrated by the figure above. The whole of the third dimension is the Life of God, spiritual Life. This life is for the purpose of transformation: changing us into the likeness of Jesus Christ.

While showing this diagram to an engineering-type friend of mine, he remarked, "The orientation of the X axis is wrong. It is always drawn from left to right." I thought about it and knew that I had shown it as the Lord had shown it to me. When I asked the Lord about it He said, "It's correct; if you are on the *inside* of it…I showed it to you from the inside of the third dimension looking out."

25

Let me put it another way. Look at this picture of an apple on the left. This apple is not really an apple; it is just a two-dimensional *representation* of the real thing. With an apple picture you can't touch the apple, feel the apple, smell the apple, taste the apple, or even hold the apple. It has no existence, no reality as an apple. Now if an artist created a beautiful glass apple, the creation would have a third dimension.

But that in itself still would not make it a real apple. What is still missing is the life of an apple, its virtue and essence of "appleness." In Christianity, the third dimension is the Life of God—His Life is the essence of the Christian's life. That is what makes Him real to us.

Missing the Mark

What is missing in both the two-dimensional diagram and the picture of the apple is reality, Life in the third dimension. For many Christians, what is missing is the presence of God in their lives; they are focused on everything but the indwelling person of the triune God—Father, Son, and Holy Spirit. In John 15, the Bible tells us that the Father is in the Son and the Son is in the Spirit and the Spirit comes to dwell in us when invited to do so.

However, if a Christian is continually distracted by the two dimensions of religion, knowledge and action, they will miss the mark of a relationship with the Triune God and will be dissatisfied with their walk. God's desire is that we would focus on Him. The enemy would draw your focus away just a bit so that you focus on the things of religion and miss the One who satisfies.

> **The Christian life that is based on knowledge *about* God or that is based on action *for* God has no reality; it is just empty religion.**

An Invitation to Life

I spent my junior year in college at the American University of Beirut in Beirut, Lebanon. This was in 1958, a very troubled time in the Middle East as the United States Marines landed in Lebanon to keep the peace. During that year in a strange and difficult environment I began to question the purpose of my existence. The question was, "Who am I and what am I for?" In response I decided to make a serious effort to "check out the God thing." When I returned to the States, I changed my major in college and prepared to attend seminary. I finished up my degree, married my true love, and we were off to graduate school at Dubuque Theological Seminary in Iowa. After completing my first year in seminary, I took a summer job with the National Council of Churches to work among migrant fruit-pickers in the Seattle area.

One Friday evening, while visiting an Episcopal church in a nearby town, we met a priest by the name of Dennis Bennett. During his evening presentation on the empowering by the Holy Spirit, Dennis said all the "wrong things" theologically; he was a conservative Christian and I was a neo-orthodox liberal. As I listened to him, I realized that the remarkable thing about Dennis was that, beyond a shadow of a doubt, he knew God personally; he had the Life of God in him and spoke of Him as an intimate friend. Sitting there in the audience, in stark contrast, I knew that I did not know God in that way.

From an early age I had always been interested in religion, active in my church, a leader in the youth group, and president of the college group at the campus Presbyterian center. However, it was all form and no substance. I longed for something more. Dennis was speaking about that "something more." My wife Trudy and I went up afterward and asked him if this "whatever you are talking about" was something we could also have. He asked me, "Are you a Christian? Have you invited Jesus Christ into your life?" For all my time in church, I couldn't remember ever doing that. He said, "Becoming a Christian is not difficult—just invite Jesus into your life. And, oh, by the way," he said, "be sure you get the power. Otherwise, it is a real drag. It is like having a brand new Cadillac car and you have to push it around all the time because you don't have any gasoline." He said, "If you are interested, just go down to the front of the church and one of my people will help you." I turned to Trudy and said, "I will if you will." And so we went.

The woman who came to us said, "So, what do you want?" I replied, "I don't know. What do you have?" Everything that had been presented that evening was completely new to me; I had no idea what they were talking about. Even though I was an intellectual at the time, I had decided this was not the place or time for an argument; I would just do the process and see what happened.

So she asked me again, "Have you ever invited Jesus into your life?" I told her I didn't know. She said, "OK, let's start there." I said the words, inviting Jesus Christ into my life. Then she said, "At this point, it is helpful to confess your sin." Well, I did have some things in my life that I was not proud of, and so I very quietly confessed them. When I was finished, she said, "Now just invite Jesus to empower you with His Holy Spirit." And so I did that, saying "Jesus, empower me with your Holy Spirit." She said, "Now you can speak in a language you have never learned…It is in the Bible and is called 'speaking in tongues.'" I opened my mouth and spoke fluently in a language I had never learned. Amazing! It was completely without emotion for me. While speaking, I analyzed the language. It had sentence structure, syntax, punctuation, and even glottal stops. When I had done this for a while, I stopped and said to her, "Is that it?" She said, "That's it."

The woman then turned to Trudy and ministered to her. Trudy had become a Christian much earlier in her life, so she just gave God permission to empower her with the Holy Spirit. That resulted in a wonderful experience that evening, and she also spoke in a language she had never learned.

But I was so disappointed! These people had told me that I was going to meet God Himself that evening, yet nothing felt different. My experience was about as exciting as tying my shoelace. About two o'clock a.m. we hopped into our little VW to drive to where we were going to stay that night. And then it happened. As I was driving, all of a sudden the presence and the peace and the joy of God filled the car and came flowing into my life. The next morning, He was still there, the awesome sense of His presence!

And so began a life of the supernatural in our Christian walk, a walk that began to unlock my heart and allow me to experience God. Trudy was so excited for me. She thought,

"Now our marriage will get even better." But it did not get better—it got more difficult. Why?

 As I took up the walk in this new life, God began to remove all of my carefully crafted theological and doctrinal religious underpinnings. Before, in seminary, I studied the Bible with literally a foot-high stack of books and commentaries on the desk. I was very much into books and books, knowledge about God and doing good for God. As these things were removed, one layer at a time, I became irritable and very unhappy. This process went on for months. During this time God made it clear that He wanted to be in charge of my education. I was going to learn of Him from Him. His guidance was that I should not read any book without His permission. He said to me, "I will teach you all things."As He removed the religious trappings from my life, He began showing me how to "know Him"—which was a very different experience from knowing *about* Him.

Being Changed
Suggested Reading: 2Timothy 3:7

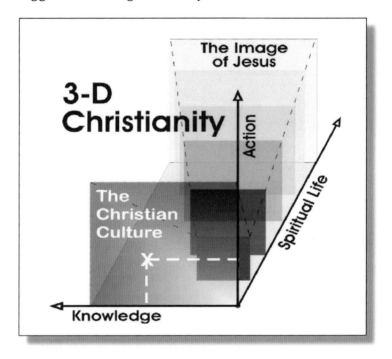

As shown in the diagram above, as I moved further into the third dimension, my knowledge of Him, my experience of Him, my communications with Him, and my life continued to change. Each of the colored planes shown inside the third dimension represents being more and more changed into His likeness. **I discovered I didn't have to be who I was; I could be who He is,** manifesting His nature into the lives of those around me and into the world.

Only then did our marriage get better. This year we celebrated our 50th wedding anniversary. And Trudy and I continue to walk in the supernatural, and He is still an ongoing presence, always with us.

So, we have been talking about how two-dimensional Christianity is missing the critical third dimension: the reality of God, the relationship with God, the Life of God. We have also looked at how endless knowledge about God and endless doing good for God does not satisfy the soul.

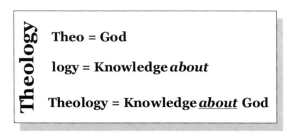

Theo = God

logy = Knowledge *about*

Theology = Knowledge <u>*about*</u> God

Only a relationship with God, the experience of Him in the third dimension of His Life, will satisfy.

The scripture in 2 Timothy 3:7 comes to mind, "...ever learning, and never able to come to the knowledge of the truth." Here, knowledge of the truth should read "an intimate knowledge of the Truth, Jesus Christ."

God's eternal purpose is to change us into the likeness of Jesus Christ. This change is based upon a relationship and obedience to a Person, not to a book or to a doctrine or to a denomination or to a religious leader. It is the continual fellowship and a walk of obedience **[Featherness]** with the Life of God that brings about the process of change. This Life only takes place in the third dimension of Christianity. It is important to move out of two-dimensional religion into Life.

Life and Lives

Suggested Reading: John 14:6, John 5:39–40, 1 Kings 17:20–23, Genesis 2:7–8, John 5:26

Let's consider a definition of "life." In John 14:6, Jesus said to Thomas, "I am the way, and the truth, and the life…" With this one statement Jesus forever defined life-- spiritual life. Life is Jesus Himself, not something  separate or apart from Him. Jesus said that the reason He came to earth was that we might have Life. In John 5:39– 40, He said to the Jews who persecuted Him, "You search the Scriptures, for in them you think you have eternal life. It is they that point to Me, but you will not come to Me that you might have life." In fact, as you read all of John 5, you will see that Jesus' whole emphasis was on Life—eternal Life, third-dimensional Life.

 In Hebrew there are two main words for life: *nephish* and *chiah*. Nephish (Strong's number 5315[3]) is a feminine noun meaning breath, life, soul- life, an animating force of a person, and, sometimes, the inner being of a person with its thoughts and emotions. It comes from the root word meaning a "puff of

---

[3] These numbers are from the *Strong's Exhaustive Concordance of the Bible*, which is an index of the King James Version of the Bible.

wind" and is used 753 times in the Old Testament. The second word for life, Chiah (Strong's number 2421), is often used as a verb meaning to be alive, to live, to keep alive; it is used at least 264 times in the Old Testament.

In the last chapter we spoke of your life being changed by the Life of God. It is clear that your life and God's Life are not the same. Let's call your life "self-life" and the Life of God "God's Life."

Self-life: Self-life corresponds to the Hebrew noun nephish—it is a created life, given by God, sustained by God, and finally removed by God. In the story of the widow whose son had died in 1Kings 17:20–23 it says:

> He [Elijah] called to the LORD and said, "O LORD my God, have You also brought calamity to the widow with whom I am staying, by causing her son to die?" Then he stretched himself upon the child three times, and called to the LORD and said, "O LORD my God, I pray You, let this child's life return to him." The LORD heard the voice of Elijah, and the life of the child returned to him and he revived. Elijah took the child and brought him down from the upper room into the house and gave him to his mother, and Elijah said, "See, your son is alive."

Here, the word *life* is nephish in the Hebrew. This was the self-life of the widow's son, given by God, taken away, and then returned. This is the soul life, the life that quickens or animates the soul of a person and causes the physical body to be alive.

God's Life: The Life of God is different and separate from self-life and is uniquely His. There is only one God's Life, and it belongs to the God of Abraham, Isaac, and Jacob. Self-life is a created life, while God's Life is not a created life but an eternal life—it has always been; it has no beginning and no end. It is God's Life that gives us eternal life if we are in Him.

Gen 2:7 וייצר יהוה אלהים את־האדם עפר מן־האדמה
ויפח באפיו נשמת חיים ויהי האדם לנפש חיה:

Consider Genesis 2:7–8: "And the Lord God formed man of the dust of the ground, and breathed into his nostrils the breath of life; and man became a living soul." According to the English translation of this passage, God breathed on Adam and gave him self-life. But if you check the Hebrew text, this is not accurate. The English translation treats the word *life* as singular: *chi*. However, in the Hebrew text the word is plural: *chiim*, or *lives*.[4] So the passage should really read, "…and breathed into his

חי **chi,** Life
חיים **chiim, Lives**

nostrils the breath of **lives**; and man became a living soul."

---

[4] If you know how to use Strong's numbers for Hebrew and Greek, you can look up the Strong's number H2421 for the word *life* in this passage. It will tell you that the word is *chi*, but if you look in the Hebrew text itself (shown in the box above), you will see that the word is really plural, *chiim*. In Hebrew the "im" part makes the word plural. One of the limitations with Strong's concordance is that it only shows you the root word, not the real word as printed in the Hebrew text.

Gen 2:17 וּמֵעֵץ הַדַּעַת טוֹב וָרָע לֹא תֹאכַל מִמֶּנּוּ כִּי בְּיוֹם אֲכָלְךָ מִמֶּנּוּ מוֹת תָּמוּת׃

What does this mean? It means that God breathed into man more than one type of life. He breathed into man both self-life and God's Life. Adam was created with two lives, his own and also the Life of God indwelling. And there is additional confirmation that Adam was given two lives at the time of creation: continue reading the narrative to verse 17. Here God says, "On the day you eat of it [the tree of the knowledge of good and evil] you shall surely die." There are two interesting things in this passage.

First, note the word *day*. In Hebrew, this word is *yom* (see the underlined Hebrew word in the text box above). This means an ordinary day of either 12 or 24 hours duration,

יוֹם **yom, day**

depending on the context of the passage where it is used. In this passage it can mean either 12 or 24 hours, but not 930 years.

You will Surely, Surely Die

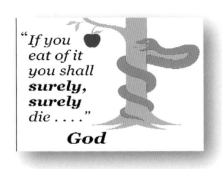

"If you eat of it you shall **surely, surely** die . . . ."
God

Secondly, in written Hebrew, there are no spaces, no vowels, and no punctuation marks. In fact, the Hebrew Bible is just one long sentence— one long string of letters written from right to left. In Hebrew, the only way to strongly emphasize a word or an action is to double the word. When you look at this passage in the Hebrew text box above, you will see that the word

36

surely is doubled. It really says, "…you shall surely, surely die." Here God is saying, "Don't doubt me on this. On the very same day that you eat of it, you really, really will die."

Now, when they ate of the forbidden tree, the tree of the knowledge of good and evil, the Bible does not record that they immediately fell down dead. In fact, it records that they continue living for 930 more years. Did God lie? God said that on that very day they would die. But they didn't physically fall down and die. When God said "you shall surely, surely die," He was speaking of His life, God's Life, being removed. They did die; they died spiritually. And, in fact, Scripture records that all people born after Adam and Eve are born spiritually dead, with only self-life.

So Adam and Eve were born with two lives: their own self-life, and God's Life. They sinned, and one of those lives—God's Life—was removed from them. All their children, and all the subsequent generations, are now born spiritually dead. There is only one exception to that consequence: Jesus Christ, the second Adam. In John 5:26 it says: "For just as the Father has life in Himself, so He has granted the Son to have Life in Himself..." Jesus was unique; He was born with the Life of God in Him. Because He never participated in sin (as the first Adam did), that Life was never removed. Jesus Christ was crucified, died, and then was subsequently raised from the dead; God raised Him from the dead. It was the indwelling Life of God that raised Him up again. Death could not hold Him because He had the Life of God indwelling.

Spiritual Life

Jesus Christ Is Life
Suggested Reading: John 14:6, Hebrews 13:5

Let's spend a moment to take another look at spiritual life, not as a philosophical or theological construct, but as a definition. Jesus said, "I am the way, the truth, and
the life…"(John 14:6). Here Jesus forever defines Life; Life is Himself. Again, Life is not something about Him, separate from him, but He Himself. He is saying "I am the Life; the Life of God dwelling in me is Life." This is the definition of Life, spiritual Life, God's Life.

Each person is born with self-life, but not God's Life. You are spiritually dead, like the first Adam, until you invite God's Life—Jesus—into your life. When He comes, Jesus brings the Life of God into your life. He comes and takes up residence in your spirit. This process of inviting Jesus into your life is called "the new birth" or "being born again" in the Scriptures. After being born again, we now have the Life of God dwelling in us also. Now we are back to square one in the Garden of Eden. If we are born again and have the Life of God indwelling, then, when we die, it is that indwelling Life of God that raises us up again into eternal life. Once the Life of God enters into us, He never leaves.

Jesus said, "I will never leave you, nor forsake you…" (Hebrews 13:5).

So what does it mean to have God's Life in us? It means everything. Having God's Life dwell in us provides the opportunity for an ongoing intimate relationship with God right now. In Romans 8:28–29 it says, "…For whom He foreknew, He also predestined to be conformed to the image of His Son, for Him to be the first-born among many brothers." In the beginning of creation, God had a wonderful plan for Adam and Eve. They were to walk with Him in the cool of the evening, having fellowship and an intimate relationship with Him. They were to eat of the tree of life in the midst of the garden, to be nourished with the Life of God, and to grow up into His likeness. They were to become like Him—manifesting His Life and His nature into the created world. That didn't happen, but God has not changed. He still wants the same relationship and intimate fellowship with us. He still wants to change us into His likeness, and He still wants us to manifest His nature into all creation.

Salvation
Suggested Reading: Hebrews 2:3, Philippians 2:12–13, Romans 5:10

Many Christians believe a doctrine that says they are made perfect when they are "born again." Does your experience indicate the truth of that doctrine? I didn't think so. Scripture speaks of salvation as an ongoing experience that *begins* with being born again. Paul speaks of a process called salvation when he says, "Work out your *own* salvation with fear and trembling; for it is God who is at work in you, both to will and to work for His good pleasure." (Philippians 2:12–13). In 1Cor 1:18, Paul again speaks of walking in Life as the process of salvation: "…but to us who are being saved it is the power of God." At the instant of our new birth, we are just the same as we were before, except that the Life of God now dwells in us. Then, as we are empowered by the Holy Spirit (sometimes called the baptism of the Holy Spirit) and we begin to give His Life access to us (that is, to our mind, our will, and our emotions), we learn to cooperate with Him in obedience, and His Life begins to change us.

Salvation is a simple concept. This is the way it works:

1) You invite Jesus Christ into your life, and He— Father, Son, and Holy Spirit—comes.
2) You give God permission to "cloth you with power from on high" and he begins to empower you for the Christian life.
3) You walk in obedience to His prompting Spirit, always available to him and allow Him to do His work in His power and in His timing in your life.

This process changes you into His image, enabling you to manifest His nature into His creation.

Knowing God in Life

Suggested Reading: Acts 17:32, 1 Corinthians 2:1–16, Phillipians 3:10, Isaiah 6:10, John 17:3, Hosea 4:6

There is knowing, and then there is *knowing*. There is knowing with the head, and then there is knowing with the heart. There is **knowing about God**, and then there is **knowing God**. In

Knowing God

It is not about knowing about God ...
It is all about knowing God.

Philippians 3:10, Paul shares with us the longing of his heart: "…that I might know Him, and the power of His resurrection…" He is not talking about a mental exercise. Paul is talking about an intimate knowledge, a knowing of the heart that comes from experiencing an intimate relationship with Jesus Christ.

Knowing *about* God is not the same as knowing God. Many Christians mistakenly believe that because they have read something, learned something, even memorized something—that because they have come to know something *about* God, that something eternal has happened in their lives. Unless it leads to an intimate relationship with God, a head full of knowledge is just doctrine, theology, philosophy, religion; it is dead, it is information without life. It is lacking the third dimension. Perhaps you have heard the saying that the longest 18 inches is between the head and the heart. The saying acknowledges that just because you know *about* something does not mean that you know it in your heart. Let's look at a few passages in the Bible that talk about knowing God.

Isaiah 6:10 speaks of knowing with the heart:

The organ for knowing is not the mind but the heart.

heart: "…they see with their eyes, and hear with their ears, and understand with their hearts…" The Hebrew word here means to perceive, to know, to understand, but the organ for knowing is not the mind but the heart.

In John 17:3, it does *not* say, "And this is life eternal, that they might know *about* you the only true God, and Jesus Christ, whom you have sent." Instead, it says, "And this is life eternal, that they might know you, the only true God, and Jesus Christ whom you have sent." It is clear that this is a knowledge of the heart in Life, and not of the head.

We have already seen 2 Timothy 3:7, "…ever learning, and never able to come to the knowledge of the truth."
Again, the statement, "knowledge of the truth' should be read "an intimate knowledge of the Truth, Jesus Christ."

In John 8:2 it does *not* say, "You shall know the truth*s* and the truth*s* will make you free." It says, "You shall know the truth and the truth will make you free." Here it is saying that we are to know the *person who is Truth* and it is He who will make you free.

Consider Paul arguing with the Athenians at the Areopagus on Mars Hill in Acts 17:32. His engaging in scholarly debate with them apparently did not lead to a life-changing encounter with God for the philosophers there; it only elicited a "come back tomorrow and we will talk about it some more" response. Paul came to realize that having an intimate relationship with Jesus Christ in the power of the Holy Spirit was far more important than elegant doctrine.

Later, Paul says to the Corinthians, "And when I came to you, brethren, I did not come with lofty words of wisdom, but with power and the Holy Ghost. For I determined to know nothing among you except Jesus Christ and Him crucified" (1 Corinthians 2:1ff).

Knowing and Doing

While discussing 3D Christianity over the phone one day, my friend said, "I understand the two levels of knowing. There is the knowing with the mind—knowing *about*—and then there is the deeper knowing that comes from doing. I really know it when I do it." But these two categories of knowing are still within the two-dimensional plane of Christian culture: Knowledge and Action. Here is an example: You read a particular Scripture and you understand it, so you know *about* what it says in the Scripture. Now you want to move into "really knowing it," so you do what it says in that passage of Scripture. Now you are doing—doing the Scripture for God, doing good for God. That is not the third dimension of Christianity, the Life of God; it is still two-dimensional Christianity, still in the plane of "knowing" and "doing." In the knowing and doing, God is not necessarily involved. All this knowing and doing can take place in just the two dimensions; it can all happen without the third dimension of God—His Life.

Consider this: when we stand before God in the final judgement, He will not ask us, "Did you get your doctrine correct and complete?" He will want to know how much of His life do we have. He will want to know how much we have been changed into the image of His Son."

Heart Knowledge versus Head Knowledge
Suggested Reading: Jeremiah 24:7, 1 Corinthians 2:14,
John 10:27, Genesis 2

I am not saying that knowledge about God is inherently
bad, only the knowledge about God that replaces or stands
in the way of an intimate relationship with Him. Our
ongoing life in Christ and our fellowship with the saints
will lead us to profound knowledge of God, as He is
revealed to us by His Spirit. Early in my life in Christ, God
told me that He would teach me all things. I took Him at
His word and determined to always try to learn only what
God Himself was teaching me. When other Christians
would share things with me, I would carefully listen, all the
while praying, "Lord, if I don't need this, let it fall to the
ground. If I don't need this for now, put it on the shelf until
You are ready to place it into my life. Or if it is for me right
now, put it into my heart and allow me to experience You
in it."

God was faithful in answering that prayer, although I found
that I normally ran about three years behind in
understanding with my head, what my heart already knew.
I would experience God in my daily life, and much later I
would think, "Oh, that is what He was doing in my life."
What He had taught me in my heart would finally be
revealed to my head.

God often speaks to me while I am taking a walk. One day
as I walked, He shared with me a very significant
revelation of Himself. I thought, "This is fantastic, I need to
remember this." Several weeks later, I was listening to the
radio and the preacher was expounding on the very same
thing that God had shown me. I was upset. "God, that's
mine. You gave it to me," I thought. "Why does he have
it?"

The Bowling Ball

In His answer, He showed me a picture of me carrying around a 16-pound bowling ball. He said, "You have taken a revelation of mine, something of Life, and have made it into a doctrine that you think you need to carry

around with you, and you feel it is something you own. In doing so, you have removed the life from it. My son, when I give you a revelation of Myself, give it right back to me, store it in me. Then it will continue to have Life. When you need it, I will give it to you again."

At other times in my early walk with God, a Christian would share with me a doctrine or a revelation or something that God was doing in his or her life. I would think, "I would really like some of that in my Christian life," and I would try to apply what they said to my life. It didn't work. I found that it was important not to help God out...only He knows how to change us into His likeness. Only He knows the *next most needful thing* for our life that will change us. If you try to take another person's experience or some head knowledge and force it into your Christian walk, you will get religion—doctrine—but you won't get life. **[Nextness]**

The Bible says that spiritual things are spiritually discerned (1 Corinthians 2:14). Only the spirit of God can teach you the things of God. In our ministry to people, we continually meet philosophical Christians; they have been convinced of the truths of Jesus Christ and have come down with a bad

46

case of mental assent. Their Christian lives do not work because they are persuaded of the *truths* of the kingdom, but they are not receiving Life and power for their walk. Only the living God can provide us with heart knowledge. Jeremiah 24:7 says, "I will give them a heart to know that I am the LORD, and they shall be my people and I will be their God, for they shall return to me with their whole heart."

Let me be clear here: I am not saying that we should not read and learn the Scriptures or be available to other Christians in fellowship. What I am saying is that we should not confuse knowledge of Scripture with Life in Christ Jesus, which comes through a relationship and an obedient walk. I treasure the revelation God has given me of Himself through the Scriptures and the knowledge and wisdom that has come out of God revealing Himself to me in my walk. Knowing God in an intimate way has allowed me to better understand what He is saying in the Scriptures.

When I read the Scriptures, I make myself available to the Holy Spirit for guidance. I ask the Spirit what He is trying to say to me. If something is unclear, I do not force the issue. I do not demand to know. In reading the Scriptures, I trust Him. In His good time, if it is important to my life, He will reveal Himself and I will come into a proper understanding.

So my concern is not about gathering knowledge in general. My concern is about accumulating knowledge and doctrine without Life; it is just religion and counts for nothing. A doctrine-driven life misses the mark. The apostle Paul had a doctrine-driven life as Saul; he was busy killing Christians as a service to God! He sincerely believed that he was doing the will of God, but he was sincerely wrong. However, even if someone's doctrine is correct, it is still a problem because a doctrine-driven life does not change us into God's likeness. It is Nothingness **[Nothingness]**. The Christian life is not all about doing good and avoiding evil; it is about obedience to a living God who speaks. "My sheep hear my voice," we read in John 10:27. The doctrine-driven life partakes of the wrong tree, the tree of the knowledge of good and evil (Genesis 2). We are called to eat of the One who is the tree of Life.

Head knowledge that substitutes for heart knowledge does not lead to Life. True knowledge comes out of an intimate relationship with Jesus Christ; then it partakes of the third dimension and has the reality of God's Life. It is knowing God that leads to Life, and obedience in Life that leads to our being changed into the likeness of Jesus Christ.

Shadows

God's Image
Suggested Reading: Genesis 2:7ff, Genesis 1:26–27

Another helpful way to look at the idea of 2D and 3D Christianity is to consider the concept of *shadow*. In the last section, we discussed that at creation (in Genesis 2:7ff), God put his Life into humans. Genesis 1:26–27 says we were created in the image of God. In that passage, God is having a conversation with Himself. He says, "Let us make man in our image, after our likeness: and so God created man in His own image, in the image of God He created him; male and female He created them." Note here that the word man refers to both Adam and Eve, male and female. Both Adam and Eve were created in God's image.

Many of us have heard sermons on this passage, and the message is often that because we are created in His image, we are little gods and we should express our little god-ness by making a difference in the world—witnessing and doing good for God. God is just like us, the message says, only bigger and more powerful. We just need to exercise our god-like-ness.

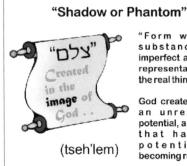

"Shadow or Phantom"

"**צלם**"

Created in the **image** of God . .

(tseh'lem)

"Form without substance, an imperfect and faint representation of the real thing."

God created us as an unrealized potential, a shadow that has the potential of becoming real.

But this passage is not telling us that we are created as little gods. In the Hebrew, the word *image* is *tseh'-lem*, which means a phantom, a shadow, a form without substance, an imperfect and faint representation of the real thing. This shadow has the potential of becoming something more. God created us as an unrealized potential: a shadow that has the potential of becoming real as He is real.

When you look at a shadow, say, the shadow of a person, you perceive a reality behind that shadow. The shadow is a two-dimensional representation of the reality that casts the shadow. Going back to the image of the apple in the former section, the

apple was just an image, a shadow, of the real thing. The real thing is an apple that has life, it has "appleness." It is three-dimensional; you can touch it, feel it, smell it, hold it, and even taste it.

You too are a shadow, but a shadow that God created to become like Jesus, to become real. God invites us, "Come and be real, come and allow me to change you into the likeness of my Son, Jesus."

Getting Real

It says in the Scriptures that God saw you before the foundations of the world, that He knows the number of hairs on your head, that He chose the time and place of your birth (Psalm 139; Luke 12:7). Who are you? You are the person God saw before the foundation of the world—you are the shadow of the reality that is in the heart of God. That reality in the heart of God is what you can become.

The Presbyterian preacher Donald Gray Barnhouse once said in one of his sermons, "God never had a thought that did not center on His Son, Jesus, and His desire is to populate the whole world with His Son Jesus." You can become part of that plan, moving from shadow into reality. God's invitation to you is, "Come, have Life, and become real as I am real."

Be Perfect
Suggested Reading: Matthew 5:48, Philippians 2:6ff, Hebrews 5:9f, John 5:19

τέλειος, téleios (Strongs G5046)

meaning finished, completed, full up.

God offers us the opportunity to be changed. What is the standard for change? "We are to be perfect, even as our heavenly Father is perfect (Matthew 5:48)." The word *perfect* here is *téleios* in the Greek, meaning "finished, completed, filled up." Even God the Son needed to be changed, completed, filled up. In Philippians 2:6ff, God the Son lays down all of His rights and prerogatives as God. He became a man, born of a woman, and entered into our world. As all other men, He was born a man with a purpose and a mission. The difference between Jesus and all other men was that He was born with the Life of God indwelling. Did you know that the Scripture does not say that Jesus Christ was perfect but says that Jesus was *made* perfect? In Hebrews 5:9f it says that Jesus was made perfect by His obedience to the Father. Then, in John 5:19 Jesus says that He can do nothing on His own; He is only doing (note present tense here) what His father is doing, only saying what His Father is saying. He had a walk to walk and a purpose to fulfill. The message of Scripture is clear. We don't have to be who we are; we can be who He is. We can have Life. We can be real.

> We don't have to be who we are; we can be who He is. We can have Life. We can be real.

52

Summary of 3D Christianity

- The evangelical Christian community is seriously fractured and is virtually indistinguishable from the secular culture.
- The Christian culture is just a reflection of the lives and hearts of the members of that culture.
- Christians are not satisfied with their walk and go searching in places that do not satisfy.
- The 2D Christian life that is based on knowledge *about* God or that is based on action *for* God has no reality. The problem with it is that if the relationship with God is missing, it is just empty religion.
- The missing dimension in the Christian Life is the third dimension which is the Life of God, spiritual Life. God's Life indwelling us is for the purpose of transformation, changing us into the likeness of Jesus Christ.
- Man was created with two lives: self-life and God's Life. Because of sin, God's Life was removed and as a consequence, all humans are now born spiritually dead.
- Inviting Jesus Christ into your life restores God's Life indwelling, an experience called being born again, which is the beginning of salvation.
- Being born again and being empowered by the Holy Spirit are essential for the Christian walk of obedience necessary for salvation.
- Knowing about God (head knowledge) is not the same as knowing God intimately (heart knowledge) as an experience.
- Store revelation in God, not as a doctrine which leads to dead religion; He will give it back when you need it.

- Reading the Scriptures under the direction of the Spirit is very important; it is one of the ways that He shows us Jesus.
- We were created as a shadow, with the opportunity to become as God is: we can be changed into the image of His Son, Jesus. This is the process called salvation.
- In the same way that Jesus was made perfect, we too are changed by our obedience to our heavenly Father.
- We aren't who we were, and we aren't who we will be. We don't have to be who we are; we can be who He is. We can be real as God is real.

The Nesses

Eight spiritual practices for
Christian transformation

The Nesses

Suggested Reading: 1 Thessalonians 5:23, Hebrews 4:12, Romans 12:2, Isaiah 6:10, Jeremiah 24:7

> **The question, then, is, "How do we get changed?"**

In asking the question "How do we get changed?" it is helpful to define what the "we" is. In 1 Thessalonians 5:23, the Bible tells us that "we" are tripartite beings; the three parts are:

- The body
- The soul
- The spirit

The Body—this is your mobile home; it is everything you can pinch.

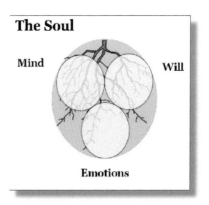

The Soul

Mind · Will · Emotions

The Soul—this is everything that makes you a unique person; your mind, your will, and your emotions; it is your thinker, your willer, and your emotor.

The Spirit—this is the receptor for spirit beings; it is the place God comes to dwell when we become a Christian. The person's spirit is also the communicator between spirit beings and the soul.

Many Christians believe the soul and the spirit to be the same thing. The Greek New Testament disagrees. Hebrews 4:12 speaks of the sword of the spirit (Jesus) dividing between the soul and the spirit, indicating they are separate and different from each other. And as discussed earlier, God's primary target for the change of the "we" is the heart (Isaiah 6:10, Jeremiah 24:7), which is both the soul and the spirit.

What does this mean in terms of how we get changed? Romans 2:12 speaks of being transformed by the renewing of our minds. The English translation says, "And be not conformed to this world, but be transformed by the renewing of your mind, that you may prove what is the good, and acceptable, and perfect, will of God."

A simple reading of this passage would indicate that if we just change our minds, the "we" will be changed and we will become like Jesus. However, this English translation of the Greek is problematic; it points in the wrong direction, focusing on the mind alone. That causes many

> **νοῦς, Nous**
>
> The soul.
> The mind, will and emotions.
> Equivalent to the heart.

Christians to read it as saying, "If you study enough, learn enough, memorize enough, and then know enough, your bad thinking will be changed; you will change your mind, and that will cause you to be like Jesus." However, that is not what it says in the Greek. The word translated *mind* here in the Greek is *nous*. It normally means the soul, which includes the mind, the will, and the emotions of a person. Often this word also means the heart—both the soul and the spirit. So the passage is really saying that our entire soul (mind, will, and emotions), and possibly our spirit as well, needs to be renewed in order for us to be transformed.

Many Christians feel that
their spiritual lives are in
a rut. Sometimes words,
doctrines, principles, and
theology keep them
trapped in that rut. They
keep doing the same
things over and over and
nothing ever changes.

That isn't the heart of
God; He has great plans for change in our lives. In this next
section we will present some new words that will help you
escape from the rut and bring new life to your Christian
walk.

Words with Life
Suggested Reading: John 6:63, John 14:12, John 5:19,
John 6:63

Do any of you speak Christianese? When we communicate
with each other, we believe they already know the
meanings of all the words they use. Over the years the

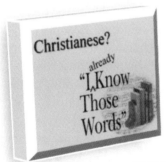

words have been filled up with
meaning—from Sunday school,
from sermons, from common
usage, from experience, etc.
However, my background and
my experience is probably is
not the same as yours, and so
my words and your words, both
with the same label, may not
mean the same thing. When we use
these words we both know what we are saying, but we may
not be communicating. For instance, one person might use
the word *salvation* to designate the born-again experience
of a Christian when God comes to dwell in a person's life.

Another person might use *salvation* to mean an ongoing process that changes us into the likeness of Jesus. They are using exactly the same word, but the meaning of the word is not the same. In addition, most Christians have a standard "Christian" vocabulary, an insider set of words that is used differently by different groups of Christian people. Often the meanings of certain words we know are just wrong; they point in the wrong direction, and they point to a wrong understanding. All of these things I call Christianese.

The words we use are important. Many of the words we use come from the Bible. However, the Bible is not King James English or NIV English—the Bible is Hebrew and Greek. When the Bible is translated from Hebrew or Greek into English, the translator often puts his or her bias into the words chosen. The selection of the English word used in translation can have a profound influence on the translated meaning of the passage. I have shown you some of these instances in earlier chapters. Later I will show you some more.

Consider the words we use. Some words seem flat, two-dimensional, and devoid of life, while others seem three-dimensional, filled with life. Jesus said that the works that He did (including speaking His Father's words), we would do also, and that we would do even greater works than those because was going to the Father (John 14:12). In the same way that Jesus only spoke what the Father was speaking (John 5:19), so also our words should come from the Spirit of God. He said in John 6:63, "…the words that I speak to you are spirit and they are life." The words we speak should also be Spirit and Life, and they will be if the Holy Spirit is speaking them through us. Our words should partake of His Life, His reality, with His power and in His timing. That changes lives.

Have you ever had this experience? Sometimes when you are sharing the good news of Jesus Christ the words don't go anywhere, they just fall to the ground and do not do the work of God. Other times they seem to hit the mark, and you see that hungry look come into the person's eyes, and they are really receptive to what God has for them. That is because sometimes we are speaking the words of God, in His timing and His power, to the person He has chosen us to speak with, and other times we miss the mark. Our timing is wrong or we are saying dead words of doctrine or the stored knowledge we have gathered over the years; good words perhaps, but not words that are Spirit and Life.

In the following section we will create some new words and fill them up with meaning. I call these words "the Nesses." The Nesses are words that encapsulate the simple things of God for our practical walk in life. They are simple, three-dimensional words that, when faithfully lived, will enable Him to bring change into our lives. The Nesses will assist you to enable Father God to do His work in you. For as Philippians 2:13 says, "It is God who is at work in you, both to will and to work for His good pleasure."

What are these words? I will begin with a few that I consider the primary words:

- Simpleness—the things of God are simple.
- Nothingness—God is the sole author of our faith and the only one that can bring change.
- Willingness—our part in the Christian walk.
- Puppyness—what it is to believe.
- Featherness—what it is to rest and obey God.
- Nextness—the path for our being changed.
- Nowness—the time for the Christian walk is only in the present.
- Forgiveness—forgive everyone, everything, all of the time, right now.

Note: The reader will notice some overlap and repetition in some of the following eight sections. They are written to be part of this book and also to be copied by you to provide "stand alone" pamphlets for limited use in your own ministry. They are also available on our website. There you will find these Nesses pamphlets as well as additional other short pamphlets that we call "Other Words to Live By."

I encourage you to read the following sections (one for each of the Nesses) slowly. Let God fill them up with meaning for you as you meditate on them—I pray that these words will be Spirit and Life to you.

Simpleness

Radical Simplicity
Suggested Reading: Romans
2:11 and 8:28f

Simpleness is the first of the
new words that we can use in
our walk in Life. Simpleness
allows us to know when we are
beginning to miss God's eternal
purpose in our lives.

A pamphlet on simpleness ought to be simple, so let's
begin.

There is often an underlying assumption in the Christian
community that the more intelligent you are, the more you
know and understand, the better Christian you are. Is that
true? Romans 2:11 says, "God is not a respecter of
persons." It says that God has no favorites. It means that no
one person has an advantage over any other person in
discovering and receiving all God is and all He has for the
people of His creation. It means that a person of great
intellect and great education does not have an advantage
over a person of little intellect or little education. Both have
an equal opportunity to receive all that God has for them.

It says in the Bible that the early disciples were ignorant
and unlearned men, yet Jesus chose each one of them. On
the other hand, the apostle Paul was a man of great
learning; yet in Philippians 3:8 he said he considered his
great learning and accomplishments under the law "as
rubbish." It is clear that our Life in Christ is not based on
our intellect or understanding.

If the Christian life isn't based on great knowledge and great learning, then it must be simple...so simple that anyone can comprehend all that is required to participate in the eternal purpose of God.

Simpleness. The things of God are simple. Be clear: if the Christian walk becomes complicated, you can be sure you are missing Him and His purpose in your life.

Prayer: Engage your heart[5] and pray: "Father, give me your eyes to see, your ears to hear, and your heart to understand all the clutter and complexity in my walk that stand in the way of my being changed into the image of Jesus. I give you that clutter and those complications; I confess I do not want them in my life. Empower me to remove the complexity from my life so I might receive everything you have planned for me in Christ Jesus from before the foundations of the world. I simply want You."

.

---

[5] "Engage your heart" means your doing Willingness, Nowness, Puppyness and Featherness.

Nothingness

Busy Doing Nothing for God
Suggested Reading: John
5:19ff, John 10:27f,
John15:1ff, John 20:21,
Philippians 4:13

Busy doing something for
God? In the eternal scheme
of things, it may all amount
to nothing.

From the very beginning of
our Christian life together, my wife and I learned that God
wanted us to live all of our lives in obedience to Him in all
things. Obedience implies that we could know the will of
God for the present moment. We began to listen for His
voice and found that He spoke to us and directed our lives.

One day, as I was out walking, He said to me, "Without Me
you can do nothing." I replied, "But Lord, look at all the
things I have done in my life without you." And He replied,
"Yes, my son, and they all amounted to nothing."

He showed me that the good stuff, the bad stuff, and all the
other stuff I did, much of it "for God," amounted to
nothing. It had no value to Him and it had no reality in the
Kingdom. Why was it of no value? Because it was "my
stuff," and often "other stuff," but not "His stuff."

A bit later in my life, I found the same message in Jesus'
teaching on the true vine in John 15. Here, Jesus tells His
disciple, "Apart from me you can do nothing."

In John 20:21, Jesus tells His disciples that in the same way that His Father has sent him, so He also is sending them. How did the Father send the Son? Jesus said that He was only doing what His Father is doing and only saying what His Father is saying (present tense). Jesus knew what His Father wanted in the moment, and He did it in His Father's timing, in His order, and in His power. Jesus walked in perfect obedience to His Father always. We too are to do what the Father is doing and to say what the Father is saying, in His order, in His power and in His timing. This is the standard for the Christian walk.

> **We too are to do what the Father is doing and to say what the Father is saying, in His order and His timing.**

If, then, without Him you can do nothing, consider that within Him ("with" Him and "in" Him) you can do all things. In Philippians 4:13, the Apostle Paul says, "I can do all things through Him who strengthens me." The Greek word for *through* in this verse is εν (en), meaning *in* or *by*. The Greek word *strengthens* is ενδυναμοω (endunamoo), to empower. We get our word dynamite from the same word. A better translation, therefore, would be, "I can do all things in (by) Him who empowers me."

We are called to seek His guidance, to be available to hear His voice, and to walk in obedience by His power in His timing. This is doing all things with Him, in Him, and by His power. This is doing what the Father is doing.

Consider the prophet Ezekiel. Once, when God spoke to him, Ezekiel was on his face before the Lord. Ezekiel 2:1–2 says, "Then He said to me, 'Son of man, stand on your feet that I may speak with you!' And when He spoke to me, the

Spirit entered into me and set me on my feet; and I heard Him speaking to me." In the Hebrew, there seems to be a pause between verses 1 and 2. It appears that God speaks to Ezekiel a second time in verse two, and as He does so, the Spirit of God enters into Ezekiel and stands him on his feet. My sense here is that Ezekiel does not immediately jump to his feet; he waits for God to empower him for whatever God wants from him.

Or consider this example: One Monday morning, God says to Bob Faithful, "I want you to speak to the person under the chestnut tree by the bridge in the park." "Got it, Lord," he replies. He immediately gets into his car and drives the 15 minutes to the park, runs to the bridge, and finds the chestnut tree. There is no one there! What happened? Bob did not do Featherness. **[Featherness]** He took the guidance and immediately made it his own to accomplish; he did not do a tentative walk of obedience, holding the guidance loosely and allowing God to do on-course correction. He did not wait for God's timing and God's empowerment. Bob arrived at the park at 10:25 on Monday morning. But God had 2 p.m. on Thursday in mind. Taking the guidance of God, and then making it your own and doing it in your own strength and timing is not the will of God for your life. It is nothingness.

John 10:27 says, "My sheep hear My voice, and I know them, and they follow Me." This is good news: we can hear His voice, and we can walk in obedience by His power and in His timing. That is doing all things with Him, in Him, and by Him...and that amounts to something.

Prayer: Engage your heart[6] and pray: "Father, my heart's desire is to hear Your voice and walk in obedience, doing only the things that You have for me to do. I don't want to spend my life doing good stuff, bad stuff, and other stuff; I want to do Your stuff instead. I don't want my life and work to amount to nothing in Your kingdom. I give You permission to speak to me, to train my heart to be available to the prompting of Your Spirit; train me to act in your timing and in your power. Lord, I want you to manifest only Your Life in my walk.

---

[6] "Engage your heart" means your doing Willingness, Nowness, Puppyness and Featherness.

Willingness

Willing the Will of God
Suggested Reading: Romans 12:2, Philippians 2:12–13, Deuteronomy 30:19

Willingness is all about learning to be available to the Spirit of God, discovering God's heart for you, and allowing Him to fulfill His purpose in your life. It is as simple as continually saying "yes" to Him.

Earlier when we discussed the soul, we indicated that it was made up of the mind, the will, and the emotions—the thinker, the emoter, and the willer. Here, we will focus on the willer.

We also learned in *Nothingness* that everything we do without Him amounts to nothing. The question then comes to mind, "So what *is* my part in the Christian walk?"

The short answer is that **our part is to choose (with our willer) the will of God for our life. It is as simple as learning to say "yes."**

The willer in your soul is like a small door. When you say yes to the intents of God, you open that little door and give God permission to do His work in you.

The longer answer is a bit more nuanced. Consider Philippians 2:12–13: "…work out your own salvation with fear and trembling; for it is God who is at work in you, both to *will* and to *work* for His good pleasure." Note that it says that God does both the willing and the work. God does the willing too? If He does the willing, then let me ask again, what is my part in the Christian walk? If He does the willing too, won't God just force His will on me and do what He wants?

Shortening the Hand of God

Father God is a gentleman; he does not force His will on us. He waits for us to be willing for His willing and His doing.

Because there is a *next most needful thing* [**Nextness**] in our lives, and only He knows what that is, we need to be willing to let Him reveal that next most needful thing in us. Then we choose the will of God for our lives and give Him permission to put that specific purpose for right now into our hearts. As we come into agreement with Him on that purpose, He is then able to begin the "doing" in our lives. That "doing" is changing us into the likeness of Jesus Christ. When we are continually willing for His willing and doing, it is called availability. We are open to Him for His good pleasure, His good purpose.

When you are unwilling, you shorten the hand of God. When you are unwilling, He will not be able to work in your life; He is not able to bless you with all the blessings he has in store for you. God waits for your willingness. A constant attitude of willingness makes us available to the Spirit of God, to hear His voice and to walk in obedience.

Two Kingdoms

There are only two kingdoms

Did you know that there are only two kingdoms: the Kingdom of God and the Kingdom of Satan? There is no kingdom of self as a third choice. In your life, you are always choosing between the Kingdom of God or the Kingdom of Satan.

If you do not choose the Kingdom of God, then by default you *do* choose the kingdom of Satan. It is your choice. You *will* choose. When you choose the Kingdom of God, you are giving Father God permission to manifest His Life in your life. The fruit of that choice is found in Galatians 5:22f: "The fruit of the Spirit is love, joy, peace, patience, kindness, goodness, faithfulness, gentleness, and self-control."

There is no kingdom of self

When you choose the Kingdom of Satan, you give Satan and his minions permission to manifest their natures in your life. The fruit of that choice is found in Romans 1:29–31and Mark 7:21–22: they are unrighteousness, wickedness, greed, evil, envy, murder, strife, deceit, malice, gossip, slander, hatred of God, insolence, arrogance, boasting, inventing evil, disobedience without understanding, untrustworthiness, unlovingness, and mercilessness, etc.

Ultimately, the Christian life is not something you do. It is not that you get strong enough to walk the Christian way. The Christian life is something God does in you. The Christian life is really God manifesting Himself in your life. When you choose the Kingdom of God—aligning your will with His will—He is the fruit of the Spirit shining out of you into His creation.

Tying it all together, the beginning of working out your own salvation is willingness. Willingness leads to availability, availability leads to obedience, and obedience leads to our being changed into His likeness, which is His good pleasure. Is it really that simple? Yes, it is; it all starts with willingness.

Prayer: Let me suggest that you come into the presence of Father God in prayer and make a clear statement (out loud) of your intent. "Father, I want to will Your will in all of my life." Then give Him permission: "Father, I give you permission to bring this into reality in my life, that I would be willing for all that you have for me in Christ Jesus. You are the only one who can, and I trust you to bring it about."

Puppyness

Be Like a Puppy

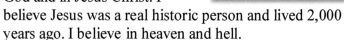

Question: Do you believe? Do you really, really believe?
Answer: Yes, I believe. I am a believer.
Question: What do you believe?
Answer: Well...I believe in God and in Jesus Christ. I believe Jesus was a real historic person and lived 2,000 years ago. I believe in heaven and hell.
Question: Excellent, but do you believe the really difficult things? Do you believe that Jesus is God come in the flesh?

Answer: Yes
Question: Well then, do you believe in the virgin birth?
Answer: Well, I'm not sure about that, but I do believe...etc.

This hypothetical exchange is familiar to most Christians, a typical discussion about believing. Many Christians are of the opinion that believing is about doctrine, that the subject of belief is a doctrinal statement consisting of a long litany of truths, and within that list of truths are certain critical core doctrines that determine your stature as a "true believer," a Christian.

In the New Testament, *believe* (πιστευω, or *pisteuo* in the Greek) is a very important word, used more than 90 times in the Gospel of John alone! But in the New Testament, the object of the verb *pisteuo* is a person, not a doctrine. The sense of the word in the Greek is reliance upon, not mere credence or mental assent. Here, *believe* points to a trusting relationship with a person—Jesus Christ—rather than just an understanding or an agreement about something.

I have a small puppy named Obadiah, a golden-white cockapoo. My puppy doesn't know anything about me; he doesn't know any of my history, who I am, what I have done, where I came from, what I do for a living, where I go to church, who my parents are, how I voted in the last elections, etc. In fact, my puppy doesn't know any "doctrine" about me. But he has an attitude about me.

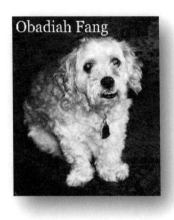

Obadiah Fang

Whenever we are in the same room, I am the center of his attention—his eyes follow me wherever I go. He follows me from room to room just to be in my presence. When I sit down in my chair, he comes to me, sits at my feet, and begs to be allowed up onto my lap. When given permission, he leaps up onto my lap and actively presents himself for my attention. Then, after I rub him behind the ears and speak to him softly, assuring him that I really care about him, he circles around once and then twice, and then his little bottom goes down, and then his front. As he settles down on my lap and is resting there, he gives a big sigh. The message is clear; "OK, I'm available...love me."

Puppy on My Lap

He is perfectly content to just rest in my presence on my lap. This attitude is not based on a litany of doctrine or a list of principles, but on a relationship, on trust. He knows that I am trustworthy, that I love him and enjoy having a relationship with him. My puppy actively seeks out that relationship and actively presents himself to be loved. He makes himself available for that relationship. This is what I call Puppyness.

Next to my big recliner chair is a long couch. Sometimes, when I am sitting in my chair working, puppy will jump onto the couch and rest there. I love having him there, and

Puppy on the Couch

he loves to be in my presence. But simply being in my presence on the couch is not the same as Puppyness—it is not the same as resting on my lap. Likewise, having God's presence in your life is not the same as resting on Him.

πιστεαυ (pisteau)
- Believe
- Have faith in
- Trust

Puppyness

Believe, or pisteuo in the Greek, is Puppyness; it is based on the trustworthiness of God and His delight in our being related to Him. *Believe* has a precise focus in the Bible: its object is God manifested in the person of Jesus Christ.

God's heart is that we be related to Him—that we come to Him, present ourselves, and say, "OK, I'm available...love me." We need to learn to snuggle down into His presence, resting on Him, allowing Him to cuddle us in His loving arms, and actively giving Him permission to love us.

Now would be a good time; seek Him in prayer and ask Him to teach you the simple skill of Puppyness.

Prayer: Engage your heart[7] and pray: "Father, lead me in the way of Puppyness. Teach me the simple skill of resting in your presence and presenting myself for your loving care." I want to experience you as love, joy, peace, patience, kindness and all you want to be to me. Father, make yourself even more real to me.

---

[7] "Engage your heart" means your doing Willingness, Nowness, Puppyness and Featherness.

Featherness

Bricks and Feathers
Suggested Reading:
Hebrews 3–4, Romans 8

Feathers float in the air, responding to every breeze. As Christians, we need to practice Featherness as the Spirit moves on us.

As I mentioned in the Nothingness section, my wife and I, at the very start of our Christian life together, learned that God wanted us to live all of our lives in obedience to Him. We began asking Him about even the small things of life, and we found He answered. This included reading the Bible under His direction. As I sat with the Bible, I would ask God, "Where do you want me to read today?" Often, He would answer me with a particular place. After a few years of reading under His guidance, He began having me read in Hebrews, specifically chapters three and four. In these chapters, God invites us to come and live in the place where He dwells, to enter into His rest, to cease from our own labors, and to dwell there. He also warns us not to harden our hearts, not to act in disobedience, and, in so doing, fail to enter into this place of rest.

You haven't gotten it yet

One afternoon, when I asked the question, "Where do you want me to read today?" the answer was still the same. He said, "Hebrews chapters three and four." I said, "Lord, you know we have been here for more than two years. I believe I understand what it says." He replied, *"Yes, but you haven't gotten it yet.* Merely understanding will not do. Until I can change you and work this into your life, we must continue here. For now, this is the *one thing most needful in your life."* And so we continued in Hebrews chapters three and four.

Hebrews 3 & 4

One day while we were reading in Hebrews chapters three and four, the Lord said, "Harden not your heart." While I had read that many times and understood what the words meant, I knew I needed to ask, and so I said, "Lord, what is a hard heart?" Immediately He showed me a picture of myself pushing against the brick wall of our fireplace. He said, "What are you doing?" I said, "Pushing against a brick wall." He said, "Is it hard?" I answered, "Yes, it is hard." He said, "Why is it hard?" He then revealed to me that it was hard because it pushed back. The harder I pushed, the harder it pushed back. Then came the lesson:

The Lord said, "During your walk with me, my Holy Spirit pushes on you with His still small voice and gentle breeze. He gives you guidance and empowers you to obey. Then, should you choose to do your own thing, you are pushing back; you are hardening your heart. Doing your own thing—pushing back—is called sin; it is disobedience." He said, "My desire for you is that you would respond to my spirit with immediate obedience." Later, God showed me that He wanted me to respond to the gentle breeze of His Spirit like a feather buoyed up by his strength, timing and direction.

I then learned that immediate obedience did not mean to grab it and run with it. It meant to stay engaged with the Spirit of God for His timing and His power. When prompted, I would begin to move as directed. However, I would hold loosely what I understood the guidance to be, acknowledging that I am hard of hearing and of slow of understanding. I call this the *tentative walk in obedience*. I allow the Spirit to do on-course correction in the direction and timing to my obedient walk.

A proper stance in the Christian walk is to constantly be available to the Spirit of God and His breath of Life. As He provides guidance for our life at the moment, we must not harden our hearts, but respond like a feather.

Respond like a feather . . .

I know that I have said it before, but because it is so important, please allow me to say it for the nth time: God's eternal purpose is to change us into His likeness. He wants to give us his Life. This only happens by obedience, and obedience implies hearing His voice. Today, when you hear His voice, don't harden your heart. Respond like a feather and be transformed into His likeness. In all things, practice Featherness.

Prayer: Engage your heart[8] and pray: "Father, you have desired to remove my heart of stone and replace it with a heart of flesh -- your heart. I give you permission to begin that process in my life right now. Teach me to enter into that place of rest, ceasing from my own labors. Father, I want to respond to you as a feather when your Spirit prompts me, that I might walk in obedience to you in all things. I give you permission to do whatever is necessary in my life to make it so."

---

[8] "Engage your heart" means your doing Willingness, Nowness, Puppyness and Featherness.

Nextness

God's Next Most Needful Thing
Suggested Reading:
Philippians 2:12, 1
Corinthians 3:12

Nextness is really a subset
of Featherness; it deals
with some additional
aspects of obedience.
Several times in this book

I have said that God has a *"next most needful thing"* for our
lives; let's look at some of the implications of it for our
walk.

Life is not only made up of a few large decisions, such as
what college to attend, your career choice, who to marry,
whether to have children, whether to buy a house, etc. Life
is primarily made up of a myriad of small decisions every
day. It is important that we are obedient to God's leading
even in these small things, because each of these decisions
closes off other life paths and opportunities for
transformation. In the "Life's Decisions" diagram below, if
you make the right turn at "1," a left turn at "2," and

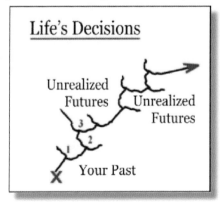

another right turn at
"3," there are a whole
series of unrealized
futures that are no
longer available. Time
moves on, and
decisions not made
have been left in the
past. When we choose
to follow our own
path, time passes,

those unrealized futures do not happen, and we are not changed. Transformation is a process; the more we are disobedient, the less we are like Him in this life. God waits for obedience—without it, there is no transformation.

Helping God is Not Obedience

Now, if we insist on helping God out by telling Him what we want and what He must do in our lives, then the change does not happen—only religion happens. God's plan is put on hold until we are willing for the *next most needful thing* for our lives. God is a gentleman. He will not force us to do His will for our lives. He waits until we are willing to follow His program.

If God is doing something in your best friend's life, and you decide He should also be doing it in your life, and you pester Him for it, that is usually a problem. That "something" is most likely not the *next most needful thing* for you; it will not change you into the likeness of Jesus. Yes, God may have that "something" also for you in your life at some point, but not next and not now. It is His program, His plan. Your part is obedience; His part is both the **willing** and the **doing** (Philippians 2:12f) in accordance to His plan. Only obedience causes you to change, and obedience is not obedience if it is out of order. If God wants A, then B, and then C in your life, and you insist on B first, then A, and then C, that is not obedience. God will wait until you are willing and ready to do A first. Then He is able to bless you with all that He has for you.

God's Plan

The plan for the process of your salvation exists only in the mind of God. He planned it for you from before the foundations of the world. If only God knows the plan, then it means that you do not know the plan. The concept of obedience to God presupposes that you do not have a plan of your own; it means that you must participate in His plan, in His timing, and by His power. That is called obedience.

Spiritual Efficiency

Consider the 1 Corinthians 3:12ff passage of Scripture that speaks of our spiritual foundations. It tells us that we can build it with gold, silver and precious stones, hay, wood and stubble. It says that on the day of judgment God will test our foundations with fire. If we have built with gold, silver and precious stones the foundation will withstand the judgment; but if we have built with hay, wood and stubble, it will be burned; there will not be anything left of the foundation; we will still be saved, though by the "skin of our teeth."

The gold, silver and precious stone here represent the increase of the person of Jesus Christ in our lives as we are changed into His image by our obedience. The hay, wood and stubble represent the product of a life spent doing good stuff, bad stuff, and our own stuff; everything but God's stuff. If we spend 44% of our time doing religion, doctrines, principles, truths and generally doing good for God – all two dimensional – and we spend 46% doing our everyday routine stuff without practicing the Nesses,. and we only spend 10% in a Life relationship with God in the third dimension of His Life, then most of our foundation is built of hay, wood and stubble and will be burned. God is calling us to walk in His Life 100% of the time, buying up the time and storing away gold, silver and precious stones. A constant practice of the "nesses" will assist in an on-going and continual relationship with God. There is a spiritual efficiency in the walk... the more we walk in relationship with God, in obedience, the more our foundation is gold, silver and precious stones

Restoration and transformation do not happen in two-dimensional Christianity— adherence to a theology or to doctrine won't do it, and doing good for God won't do it; only the Life of God in our lives and a walk in obedience in three-dimensional Christianity can make it happen. Only God knows the plan; only God knows what must come next. The Christian life is a series of *next most needful things* in obedience to God's prompting. It is Him executing His plan in our lives by His Life in the third dimension. That is Nextness.

Prayer: Engage your heart[9] and pray: "Father God, I give you permission to show me the *next most needful thing* in my life. Share your heart with me and provide me with that inner witness of your Spirit that this is the way of Life. I want to will both Your **willing** and Your **doing**. Forgive me for all the wasted time in my life when I have been disobedient to you. I give you irrevocable permission to deal with everything that the enemy has added to my life, and I give you permission to change me into the likeness of your Son, Jesus. Father, I want Nextness in my life."

---

[9] "Engage your heart" means your doing Willingness, Nowness, Puppyness and Featherness.

.

Nowness

Life in the present tense
Suggested Reading: Deuteronomy 30:15–20

To paraphrase Deuteronomy 30:19, God is saying to us, "I have set before you this day Life or death, my blessing or the curse of my enemy Satan…*Now* choose life that you may live, by loving Me, by obeying My voice, and by holding fast to Me; for I am your life." Let's look at the idea of "now."

The Now

- Now refers to an infinitely small segment of time that contains only the present tense.
- Now does not contain any past.
- Now does not contain any future.
- Now is the only time you have.
- Now is the only place choice can happen.
- Now is the only place you can have Life.

The Not-Now

The not-now has only two dimensions: the past and the future. It has no present. The enemy of God would rob you of the now by focusing you on the past in self-pity, bitterness, unforgiveness, resentment, etc., or focusing you on the future through fear of what might happen; he would have you continually asking, "what if?" to keep you afraid of the future.

Choose Now

God created us for relationship. Now is the only place of relationship and fellowship with God, with others, and with yourself. You can't have a relationship  with someone in the future or in the past. Now is the place you live, the place of Life, the place of being available to God for His purpose in your life. Now is the place where you discover the *next most needful thing* [Nextness] God has for you.

Jesus said, "I came that you might have life." That life only takes place in the present. The whole of the Christian walk, including three-dimensional Christianity and the Nesses (Simpleness, Nothingness, Willingness, Puppyness, Featherness, Nextness, Nowness, and Forgiveness) all happen in the "now."

God would have you fully present in the now: available to Him, responsive to Him, obedient to Him. He communicates with you only in the present, and He loves you in the now. You can only love God, others, and yourself in the now. Now is where you touch the heart of God, see His face, know His heart, know His love, discover His will for your life, walk in obedience, and finally are changed into his likeness. Choose now.

Prayer: Engage your heart and pray: "Father, I confess that I want to live and have Life in the now. I don't want to escape into the enemy's kingdom—the past or the future. I really want all you have for me in the now. I choose Life; I choose now. Change my heart to always desire the now. I give you permission to teach me Nowness."

Forgiveness

Forgiving everyone, everything, all of the time, right now.

Suggested Reading: Matthew 6:14–15, Luke 17:4, 1 John 1:9, Romans 12:19, Proverbs 19:5

Matthew 6:14–15: "For if you forgive men their trespasses, your heavenly Father will also forgive you; but if you do not forgive men their trespasses, neither will your Father forgive your trespasses."

1 John 1:9: "If we confess our sins, He is faithful and righteous to forgive us our sins and to cleanse us from all unrighteousness."

Forgiving is so important; it is foundational to the Christian life. But when we have a spirit of unforgiveness in our hearts it says, "I am not willing to forgive the offense against me. I will remember what has been done to me. I will never forgive that person."

> **Forgiveness**
>
> **It is not a suggestion; it is a commandment.**

It is clear from Matthew 6 that forgiveness is not optional. It is not just something you do if you feel like it—it is absolutely essential to the process of dealing with the sin in your own life. Forgiveness is your key to freedom. If you do not forgive, then God will not forgive you and free you from sin and guilt. To get that freedom, you must participate in all four aspects of forgiveness.

The Four Aspects of Forgiveness
1. Forgive those who have wronged you.
2. Ask forgiveness from those you have wronged.
3. Forgive yourself.
4. Forgive God??

Forgive Those Who Have Wronged You

Forgiving others is releasing someone from the wrong they have done to you. It is agreeing with God that they no longer owe you something for the wrong done. It is important to forgive as soon as God brings someone to your attention. However it is important to realize that forgiving someone is a process; it is not accomplished in just a single moment.

That process goes like this: Through God's prompting you remember someone you need to forgive. You say the words of forgiveness, not just with your head, but engaging your heart as much as you are able. It is important to be specific. For example, you might say, "Father God, I forgive Ms. Hurtme for her hurtful behavior toward me at the company Christmas party last year." And then follow up with, "And Father God, I give you permission to bring this forgiveness to completion in my heart." Then include that person in your prayers. You initiate the prayer and indicate your willingness to forgive, but only Father God can bring your forgiveness to completion—all the way to blessing them.

Ask Forgiveness From Those You Have Wronged

In the same way that you must forgive, you must also ask forgiveness from those you have wronged—and in some instances make restitution. Go before the Spirit of God and allow Him to show you any person you have wronged and the nature of your offense.

Now, seek His wisdom for the time and the method of asking forgiveness of them and how to make right the wrong, if necessary. Then be obedient, ask their forgiveness, and if required, make restitution. If they will not forgive you when you ask, know that you have done what is required, and you are released. If they do not forgive you, then it remains as sin in their life -- it is no longer your sin.

Sometimes it is not possible to ask the person for forgiveness (for example, if you don't know where they are or if they are deceased), or God might indicate that it is not appropriate to ask their forgiveness. If that is the case, then just ask for God's forgiveness for having wronged them, and then let it go.

Forgive Yourself

The enemy of God, Satan and all his minions, is called the accuser of the saints. He would attempt to ruin your life with the burden of guilt. Be sure that, as you are forgiving others, you also remember to forgive yourself and release to God the burden of guilt that you carry.

Forgive God??

This is a very hard thing for Christians to understand. Why would you need to forgive God? He is perfect and isn't guilty of anything. So why would a Christian have bitterness (an unforgiving, resentful, angry attitude) against God?

A few years ago a pastor came to me for ministry. He told me he had a very successful ministry; in his church God had often used him for many supernatural things, like healings and prophecy. He said that he had always had a strong sense of God in his life. But then he told me that all of that had gone away, and nothing worked anymore. After our second session, it was clear why his ministry and his life were in trouble: he had a deep resentment against God for some things that had happened to him—he blamed God. He felt that God had wronged him and had caused the loss of "success" in his ministry and all of the pain in his personal life.

Do you have bitterness against God? Do you resent or feel angry with God, or do you feel He has let you down and not kept his promises to you, that He is responsible for your problems? You may know in your head that God is not guilty, but your heart says otherwise. Your heart says, "Where were you when I needed you?" and "Why did you allow this to happen to me?" Sometimes you even blame God for the times you felt certain that God had promised you something and He has not yet delivered. Sometimes, our hearts blame God that He feels absent from our lives, or that He is responsible for the hurts of the past.

Proverbs 19:3 illustrates the point: "When the foolishness of man ruins his life, his heart is angry against God." Are you blaming Him for your own foolishness? The enemy of God -- Satan, is called the accuser of God; he wants you to blame God. When you cooperate with him, the resulting bitterness is a door point for him to gain additional access to your life.

Now, returning to the story: I shared with this pastor that God had not caused these things; they were the work of the enemy of God, Satan. The enemy had then led him astray by telling him that God had caused the problems. The pastor cooperated with the enemy and believed the lie, forming bitterness in his heart toward God. So it wasn't that the pastor needed to forgive God for the bad things God had done to him—he needed to deal with the sin of cooperating with the enemy and the sin of bitterness, and then he needed to ask God's forgiveness. Nothing was going to change in his life until he repented and dealt with his sin. By our fourth session, the pastor agreed that he had indeed sinned against God. He repented of his sin and asked God's forgiveness. The pastor's life began to be restored.

If you have bitterness against God, first deal with the sin and then seek God's forgiveness.

The Standard for Forgiveness

Luke 17:4: "And if he sins against you seven times a day, and returns to you seven times, saying, 'I repent,' forgive him."

> **Everyone, Everything, All of the Time, Right Now**

What is the standard of forgiveness? God's standard for forgiveness is that we must forgive everyone, everything, all of the time, right now -- completely, all the way to blessing.

There are three steps to forgiveness:

- Say "Father, I forgive (person) for (what) at (where) on (time or date)." Be specific.
- Then pray, "Father, I give you permission to bring this forgiveness to completion in my heart."
- Then continue to pray for the person and allow God to change your heart to the point where, over time, you can genuinely extend blessing to them.

For instance, "Father God, I forgive my pastor for the statements he made about me at the board meeting last week," and, "Father, I give you permission to bring this forgiveness to completion in my heart." Then continue to pray for that person.

The next time you think of that person or see that person, if there is still a sharp bite in your spirit, continue with the three steps. How often do you do this? The Scripture says we should do this seventy times seven times, which basically means we need to do it as often and as long as it takes.

Forgiveness Is a Process

How do you know when you have forgiven? Forgiveness is not a carwash; it is a process and a heart matter. Only God can bring it to completion. Often when you forgive someone, it feels like not much has happened. You think, "I have forgiven the person, but I surely don't want to ever see or talk to them again!" You are not done yet. But as you continue the process, you find yourself changing; God is changing your heart. You continue to forgive them. After a while, the sharp bite goes away and you think, "Okay, now I have forgiven them. I actually would be willing to see them again." You still are not quite finished. God's standard is that your forgiveness would go all the way to blessing-- forgive again and again until you can look the person in the eye and truly ask God's blessing on them. When you can say in your heart, "I truly would like to bless that person" and mean it, then you have come all the way to forgiveness. God is not asking you to forget, just to forgive. You'll probably always remember the wrong done to you, but once you have forgiven, you no longer need to carry it as a sin in your own life. And in terms of wrongs you've

done to others, your freedom does not depend on them forgiving you; it only depends on you sincerely asking for forgiveness.

Justice Is God's Alone

Many Christians think, "But if I forgive that person, they get away with the wrong they did to me. I want justice!" Romans 12:19 makes it clear to us that we are not to become angry and extract satisfaction by punishing the person who wronged us. God is protecting us by telling us that He will take care of it. "'Vengeance (justice) is

Let Yourself
Off The Hook

Mine,' says the Lord, 'I will repay them.'" When you forgive someone, you get off the hook; they don't. God no longer holds you accountable for the sin of unforgiveness, but God still holds them accountable for their sin.

"Not forgiving is like drinking rat poison and then waiting for the rat to die."[10]. Only you are poisoned; they are not affected by your unforgiveness. Unforgiveness slowly, like poison, takes your Life—your spiritual Life.

Begin the Process

Let me suggest an orderly approach to forgiveness. Take a full sheet of paper and at the top make five columns. Label them Who, What, When, Where, and 70x7.

Who	What	When	Where	70 X 7

Prayer: Now spend time in prayer. Engage your heart and ask God to show you any unforgiveness in your life. Write down the names of the people involved, the wrong they did (or the wrong you did to them), when this happened as best as you can remember (make the event specific—you may have a number of items for just one name), and where it happened.

Then say "Father, I forgive (person) for (what) at (where) on (time or date)." And, "Father, I give you permission to bring this forgiveness to completion in my heart." Then continue to pray for that person.

As God brings others to mind, just add them to the list and continue as needed. You will be amazed by His faithfulness in forgiveness.

---

[10] Anne Lamott, *Traveling Mercies*

Nesses Summary

- God's eternal purpose is that we should be changed into the likeness of Jesus Christ.
- The "we" that gets changed is our soul plus our spirit; the combination is called the spiritual heart.
- We can allow God to fill up the words we speak with His Life; then they become Spirit and Life when spoken.
- The Nesses are eight simple three dimensional words which, when they are faithfully lived, allow God to bring change into our lives--changing us into the likeness of Jesus and fulfilling the eternal purpose of God.
- **Simpleness:** The things of God are simple. When the Christian walk becomes complicated, we can be sure we are missing Him and His purpose in our lives.
- **Nothingness:** Everything we do without God amounts to nothing; with Him and in Him we can do all things.
- **Willingness:** Our part in the Christian walk is to be willing for God's willing and doing. God is a gentleman and will not force His will on us; we are called to choose His kingdom and His righteousness (Jesus), and then all that He has for us is added into our lives.
- **Puppyness:** The word "believe" in the Bible has a precise focus; its object is God manifested in the person of Jesus Christ. To believe is to do Puppyness--the simple practice of resting on God and making ourselves available for His loving care.

- **Featherness:** Featherness is not hardening our hearts but instead entering into that quiet place of His presence, ceasing from our own labors, making ourselves available for the still, small voice of His Spirit, and responding like a feather in obedience, in His timing and His power.
- **Nextness:** God has a plan from before the foundations of the world to *transform* you into the likeness of His Son, Jesus, and to *restore* the you by removing the enemy from your life. That plan involves your cooperating with God in His *next most needful thing* in your life. Don't help Him out; only He knows the plan and the timing for your life.
- **Nowness:** Life in God does not take place in the past or in the future; all of our Life in God takes place in the now.
- **Forgiveness:** God's standard is that we would forgive everyone, everything, all of the time, right now. Forgiveness is not a suggestion, it is a commandment. Forgiveness is not a carwash, it is a process and takes time to complete. God will not forgive you if you do not forgive others. Forgiveness is absolutely foundational to the Christian walk and is the key to spiritual freedom in our lives.

Finis

So now, after several cups of tea, the candle is burning low and the cookies are almost gone. With perseverance, you have come to this point in our little book. Together, we have spent considerable time in chapter nine and have moved onto the Nesses as helpful and important practices for transformation in our Christian walk. I encourage you to try them; you will like the change He brings about in your life.

The promise of God is clear: We don't have to be who we are; we can be who He is. We can have Life. We can be real.

I pray that you will enter into the rest of God and allow Him to bless you with every blessing that He has purposed for in you in Christ Jesus from before the foundations of the world, that you would receive a clear vision of God's eternal purpose and come to know the love of God and the joy and peace of being changed into His likeness, that the words you speak might be spirit and life with the power to change.

And finally I pray, as Paul did in Ephesians, "that He would grant you, according to the riches of His glory, to be strengthened with might by His Spirit in the inner man; that Christ may dwell in your hearts by faith; that you, being rooted and grounded in love, may be able to comprehend with all saints what is the breadth and length and depth and height, and to know the love of Christ which passes knowledge, that you might be filled with all the fullness of God. Now to Him who is able to do exceeding abundantly above all that we ask or think, according to the power that works in us, to Him be glory in the church by Christ Jesus throughout all ages, forever. Amen." (Eph 3:16-21 MKJV)